J.C Platt

Reminiscences of The Early History

of Dark Hollow, Slocum Hollow, Harrison Lackawanna Iron Works,

Scrantonia and Scranton, Pa.

J.C Platt

Reminiscences of The Early History
of Dark Hollow, Slocum Hollow, Harrison Lackawanna Iron Works, Scrantonia and Scranton, Pa.

ISBN/EAN: 9783337125387

Printed in Europe, USA, Canada, Australia, Japan

Cover: Foto ©Andreas Hilbeck / pixelio.de

More available books at **www.hansebooks.com**

REMINISCENCES

OF

THE EARLY HISTORY

OF

DARK HOLLOW, SLOCUM HOLLOW, HARRISON LACKAWANNA IRON WORKS, SCRANTONIA

AND

SCRANTON, PA.

✧ ✧ ✧

READ BEFORE THE LACKAWANNA INSTITUTE OF HISTORY
AND SCIENCE, NOVEMBER 9, 1886,

BY J. C. PLATT.

✧ ✧ ✧

SCRANTON, PA.:
THE REPUBLICAN, LITHOGRAPHING, PRINTING AND BINDING.
1889

Reminiscences of the Early History

"DARK HOLLOW," "SLOCUM HOLLOW," "HARRISON," "LACKAWANNA IRON WORKS," "SCRANTONIA," AND "SCRANTON, PA."

———

READ BEFORE THE LACKAWANNA INSTITUTE OF HISTORY AND SCIENCE, NOV. 9, 1886.

———

r. President, Ladies and Gentlemen :

It is with great diffidence that I have made an ,ort to respond to the request to prepare a paper or this Society on "the early history of Scran-pn"—which is herein understood to include only territory which formed the borough of Scran- and not the entire city,—for there have been eady published not less than a dozen histories[*] .f the Wyoming and Lackawanna Valleys and 'Scranton, and I have been compelled to repeat much matter that has already appeared—a considerable portion of which I originally furnished.

The early history of this portion of the coal

———

[*]Miner's, Stone, Peck, Chapman's, Pierce, Hollister's 3 editions, White's 3 editions, Gallatin. Clarke, Mussell & Co.

basin is so closely connected with that of Wyoming, that it is difficult to separate them ; and to separate the history of the "Iron Works" from that of Scranton itself is impossible.

Connecticut by its charter, (granted in 1662,) covered the forty-second degree of latitude and extended "from Narragansett river on the east to the South sea on the west," excepting such lands as were then occupied by prior settlers ; namely, New York and New Jersey.

Nearly nineteen years afterwards Wm. Penn obtained a grant of lands on the west side of the Delaware river extending northward to the forty-third degree of latitude ; this covered a part of the territory embraced in the Connecticut charter.

Miner's history states that in 1762 a considerable number of emigrants had arrived in Wyoming Valley from Connecticut and "after sowing grain they returned to their families, with whom, early in the following spring, they came back."

Pierce's annals state that "the first settlers from Connecticut, who came to New York, (coming in 1762 and 1763,) crossed the Hudson river at or near Newburgh and, proceeding westward, passed the Delaware river at its junction with Shohola creek. From this point they followed an Indian path along Roaring Brook to the Lackawanna river, and thence by another Indian path to the place of destination. The emigrants of 1769 followed the same route, but being accompanied by carts drawn by oxen, they were compelled to use the axe ; and from this period we date the first wagon road from the Delaware to the north branch of the Susquehanna.

The late Mr. Allen Secor told me some years since, that the old road did not run through Dunmore corners, but nearly east from where the street railway to Dunmore now passes under the Erie and Wyoming Railroad Company's branch from Number Six to Scranton.

⁚. It appears to be generally understood that about 1786 or 1788, Phillip Abbott from Connecticut, built a log house near Roaring Brook (on some of the old maps " Gully Creek,") a little below where the old Red House (built by Ebenezer Slocum) stood. That not long afterwards he built a small grist mill* near the old Grist Mill dam, which dam was in use until August, 1885, when it was carried away by a freshet and abandoned. Steam power is now used to run the mill.

---

*Since the above was read before the Institute, I have met Rev. J. D. Waller, of Bloomsburg, who says that Ashber Waller—a local Methodist preacher who afterwards moved to Ohio—" built the first flouring mill on the Lackawanna."

The father of J. D. W., then living at what is now South Wilkes-Barre, helped raise the mill. He came up with an ox team and took back pine lumber to use in a house he was then building.

James Abbott became interested with his brother Phillip, in October of the same year, and Reuben Taylor in 1789. In 1790 John Howe purchased the mill of Abbotts & Taylor, and doubtless the land, for Mr. Joseph Slocum (now residing in our midst at the ripe age of 86, with his mind as clear as ever), says that his father, Ebenezer Slocum, purchased his land of John Howe in 1797 and moved his family here from Wyoming Valley in 1798.

Mr. Joseph Slocum was born in 1800, in Wilkes-Barre, when his mother was there on a visit.

The first name of the place was Dark Hollow, Ebenezer Slocum named it Unionville, but it soon became known as Slocum Hollow and successively Lackawanna Iron Works, Harrison, Scrantonia and finally Scranton.

The "Old Red House,"—which stood about seventy-five or one hundred feet west of the westerly corner of the grain mill, built by Scrantons & Platt in 1850, and now standing—was built by Ebenezer Slocum in 1805 and occupied in 1806. It was the first frame house built in this neighborhood and was torn down in May, 1875, to make more room for the steel works of the Lackawanna Iron & Coal Co.

What is now the blast furnace dam was first

built by Ebenezer Slocum and James Duwain (or Duane), in 1799, for an iron forge which was erected near it. The dam was soon carrried out by a freshet, which discouraged Mr. Duwain. Mr. Slocum's brother, Benjamin, succeeded Mr. Duwain as a partner in the iron business, and in 1800 the dam was rebuilt.

In 1828 Joseph Slocum rebuilt the dam and with his brother, Samuel, built a saw mill which was removed by Scrantons, Grant & Co. to make room for the first blast furnace built here—" old Number One."

During 1885 and 1886 the L. I. & C. Co. built a solid cut stone dam in the same place, which will probably withstand all future freshets.

The partnership of Ebenezer and Benjamin Slocum was dissolved in 1826, and the latter removed to Tunkhannock.

Mr. Ebenezer Slocum died here July 25th, 1832, and his brother Benjamin, in Tunkhannock, on the 5th of the same month.

The Slocums commenced distilling whisky about the time the forge was built—1799.

The old stone house under the hill and near the old grist mill, was known as the " lower distillery." This building was taken down in April, 1854, by the L. I. & C. Co. to build a retaining wall where it stood. A wooden building which stood where numbers 2 and 3 furnaces are now, was known as the "upper distillery," and Mr. Benjamin Slocum lived in the upper part of it. This building was taken down by Scrantons & Platt in 1848 to make room for building the above furnaces. Both of these buidings were used as residences when I moved here in 1846, and until they were taken down.

The last whisky was made in the "upper distillery" in 1824, and in the lower one in Dec. 1826. The last iron was made in the old forge, June 10, 1822, and Mr. Joseph Slocum has carefully preserved the old hammer that was used to make it.

POSTOFFICE.

The first postoffice in this township was established here* January 10th, 1811, under the name of "Providence." Its location here is the best of evidence that it was then, as now, the business centre of this neighborhood, doubtless owing to its grist and saw mill, iron forge and distilleries.

I am indebted to Hon. Joseph A. Scranton for a late letter from Third Assistant Postmaster General, A. D. Hazen, which states that the postoffice

---

*It should be noticed that though the name of the postoffice was "Providence" from the first, it was really first located in what became Scranton, and was removed to Providence corners by Mr. Vaughn, thus leaving the old locality without a local postoffice for some time prior to the spring of 1850.

at Unionville was established Jan. 10, 1811, under the name of " Providence," and the Hyde Park postoffice July 14, 1832, and both continued under their respective names until merged into the carrier delivery of Scranton, Oct. 22, 1883. Also that the office of " Scrantonia " was established April 1, 1850, and changed to " Scranton " Jan. 23, 1851.

Mr. Calvin Washburn and family moved to Hyde Park in 1820. He purchased half of the Bowman estate, 156 acres, for $885, or $5.67 per acre. About 1858 he sold the same for $250 an acre. His son, Nicholas Washburn, tells me that he remembers when the only postoffice in this township was at Unionville, and Mr. Benjamin Slocum the postmaster; that the mail was carried on horseback, the route being from Pittston up the centre or main road to Hyde Park, thence over the only bridge crossing the Lackawanna river between Old Forge and Carbondale— at the same place where the present one is near the gas works—to Unionville (Providence P. O.), then back to Hyde Park ; thence via Providence village, or Centreville, the "Ten-Mile Tavern" and Clifford turnpike to Dundaff.

Mr. Norval D. Green, now residing on Jefferson avenue with his son, D. N. Green, says that Benjamin Slocum, the postmaster at Unionville, resigned his office in favor of Mr. John Vaughn,

Jr., who received the appointment and removed the office to "Providence Corners," or Razorville or Centreville*, and Mr. Green attended to the mail business, opening the first mail received there.

Mr. Edward Merrifield states that his father, the late Hon. Wm. Merrifield, was the first postmaster at Hyde Park when it was established July 14, 1832, and held it about a month, when he moved out of the place, and *his* father, Robert Merrifield, was appointed to succeed his son. Later Mr. Wm. Merrifield returned to Hyde Park, and was reappointed June 5, 1834.

Mr. Oliver P. Clarke, now residing in Hyde Park, states he moved there in April, 1846, was made postmaster in June of that year, and removed the office from Judge Wm. Merrifield's store, which stood nearly opposite the present brick M. E. church on Main street, to the store of Clarke & Blackman, on the easterly side of "Fellows' Corners," where he kept it until 1856, when he removed it to his new store on Main, at the head of Scranton street. Mr. Clarke was succeeded in 1857 by Doctor S. M. Wheeler.

In the winter of 1847 and 1848 a census was taken to show the necessity of a postoffice at this place. Mr. O. P. Clarke, postmaster, as stated, at

*See note on page 8.

Hyde Park, gave a written statement showing that
seven-tenths of the mail matter received at his
office went to Harrison, or the Lackawanna Iron
Works. The petition asked to have Dr. B. H.
Throop made postmaster, but President Polk's
Postmaster-General ignored the application.

Another effort was made during the session of
Congress for 1849–50, which resulted in the estab-
lishment of an office under the name of Scrantonia, and the late John W. Moore was made postmaster. The writer took the first letter and paper
from the office when it opened, April 1, 1850.

The office was in the front room of Mr. Moore's
tailor shop, and is now standing, being the first
building easterly from the Iron Company's old
store and office—now car and smith shops—near
the blast furnaces.

It may be the impression that the Messrs.
Scranton were instrumental in having the place
named after them, but such is not the fact. The
subject was being discussed by the Rev. J. D. Mitchell and myself, and I suggested to Mr. Mitchell
that as he was acquainted with the Hon. Chester
Butler, then member of Congress for this district,
that he should write to him and state that it was
thought by their friends they were entitled to the
compliment. There was no objection made, and
the office was called Scrantonia. At a meeting of

those interested in the iron works, including gentlemen from New York and Connecticut, held here during the next autumn, a motion was carried unanimously that the last two letters of the name be cut off, leaving it Scranton.

FIRST RAILROAD PROJECT.

1826   The Susquehanna and Delaware Canal and Railroad Company's charter was approved April 3, 1826.

Messrs. Henry W. Drinker, Wm. Henry and James N. Porter appear to have been prominent members of the commission to open the books.

The charter authorized subscriptions for 30,000 shares at $50 each, making a capital of $1,500,-000, with authority to increase it if needed; to make a canal or railroad, or part of each, from the mouth of the Lackawanna river to a point on the Delaware at or near the Water Gap, and to a point on the river near to Durham creek, in Bucks county; also a branch railroad or canal to Wilkes-Barre, with a proviso that no dam should be erected in either the Susquehanna or Delaware rivers.

Conductors of wagons or vehicles of any kind were to blow a trumpet or horn one-quarter of a mile from the collector's office, to notify him to be ready to take the toll. The company was authorized to collect, in the aggregate, up to twelve per centum per annum on the capital.

It was provided "that said railroad shall, in no part of it, rise above an angle of two degrees with the plane of the horizon." (Two degrees is a little over 185 feet per mile.)

The "Liggett's" Gap railroad charter was approved April 7, 1832. 1832

It is very evident that this road, like its predecessor of 1826, was to be run on the canal method, every one using it to furnish his own vehicle and power for transportation—presumed to be horses.

The tolls authorized, were two cents per ton, per mile, except on lumber, coal, salt and plaster, which were one-half cent per ton less ; the same to be paid before the vehicle could proceed further, the conductor to be fined $20 for violation of this rule.

Of the sixteen commissioners named, Messrs. Henry W. Drinker, Jeremiah Clarke, Nathaniel Cottrell, Thomas Smith and Dr. Andrew Bedford —the latter the only one now living—appear to have taken the most interest in the enterprise. If my recollection is correct, the only commissioners present at the organization of the company at Kressler's hotel, January 2, 1850, were Messrs. Drinker, Bedford, Clarke and Smith.

This hotel stood where the north boilers of the blast furnaces are now located.

I have in my possession the original minutes of the meeting alluded to above, signed by H. W. Drinker, Chairman, and John S. Sherrerd, Secretary.

1836   Somewhere about 1836, Messrs. William Henry, of Stroudsburg; H. W. Drinker, of Drinker's Beech; Edward Armstrong, residing about six miles above Newburgh on the west side of the Hudson river; and Lord Charles Augustus Murray, (a Scotchman and son of the Earl of Dunmore,) became interested in the question of the proposed Susquehanna and Delaware Canal and Railroad Company scheme.   Their plan was to have a canal or slackwater navigation from the mouth of the Lackawanna to what is now Scranton and a railroad from here to Port Colden, N. J., and there connect with the Morris Canal, which was open to New York.

In this way they secured the favorable influence of Mr. Edward Biddle who had been United States Senator, and of Samuel L. Southward, who was then President of the Morris Canal.

Lord Murray was on a visit to see this new country and made a number of hunting trips with Mr. Armstrong to and over the Moosic mountains

for grouse and other game, and thus became interested in the plan and route.

There are those yet living in this region who
remember both of these gentlemen and their fine
hunting dogs.

During the Scotchman's visit he made the acquaintance of Miss Wadsworth, of Geneseo, N. Y.,
and afterwards married her. Her grave is in the
grounds of the Wadsworth Mansion at Geneseo.

Mr. Drinker was instrumental in having our
neighboring borough called Dunmore, in compliment to his friend, Lord Murray.

The railroad company was organized, and Lord
Murray was empowered and expected to raise
$1,500,000 to build it. The projectors were so
sure the road would be built that a farm was purchased not far above the Water Gap for railroad
shops, &c.

In July, 1840, Mr. Henry commenced negotia-
tions with Messrs. Wm. Merrifield, Wm. Rickitson
and Zeno Albro for a 503 acre tract of land " on
which was a saw mill and two small dwelling
houses, about 50 acres cleared, balance covered
with pine, hemlock and oak timber," that formerly
belonged to Ebenezer Slocum, deceased. Mr.
Armstrong was to have been interested with Mr.
Henry in this purchase.

On the return of Lord Murray to England it

1840

was said his cousin, Queen Victoria, prevailed upon him to decline making any investments in America, the result being fatal to the railroad project.

The Queen afterwards made him her envoy to Persia and still later her minister to Saxony.

FIRST PURCHASE BY THE PREDECESSORS OF THE LACKAWAWANNA IRON AND COAL CO.

1840   About the time Mr. Henry had concluded his engagement to take the land of the Hyde Park gentlemen, Mr. Armstrong was called home by the sickness of his two daughters, was taken sick himself and died.

This left the contract for the Scranton land resting upon Mr. Henry, who then interested his son-in-law, Mr. Selden T. Scranton, who induced his brother, George W. Scranton, and Mr. Sanford Grant to accompany Mr. Henry and himself to "Lackawanna" to see the "promised land," the result being that these gentlemen assumed the contract August 20, 1840. The deed is dated September, 1840, consideration $8,000, or about sixteen dollars per acre.

About three-quarters of Lackawanna avenue is on this tract, and the remainder on a tract purchased February 8, 1847, of Messrs. Gillespie and Pierce and Barton Mott, on which stood the old wood grist mill and its dam.

At the date of the first purchase, in 1840, there were here five dwellings, one school house, one cooper shop, one sawmill, one grist mill.

Somewhat later Mr. Philip H. Mattes, of Easton, examined the property and took an interest in the concern, when the firm of Scrantons, Grant & Co. was organized with a capital of $20,000, Messrs. George W. Scranton, Selden T. Scranton, Sanford Grant and Philip H. Mattes being the partners.

In October, 1840, Mr. Wm. Henry moved from Stroudsburg to Hyde Park, occupying a house on the north side of Fellows' Corners, and took charge of the early operations.

Mr. Simon Ward says he came here on Sept. 8, 1840; that Mr. Henry being absent he looked up some tools and commenced work on the 11th, getting out stone for the first blast furnace, about where the east boilers of the blast furnaces now stand. He also states that the school house then standing at the top of the hill northeasterly from the grist mill had just been finished and soon opened with seven scholars. Jos. Slocum sent one, Samuel Slocum two, Jos. Hornbacker one, Barton Mott one, Ebenezer Hitchcock two.

First Blast Furnace.

Mr. Wm. W. Manness arrived here on the 2nd day of September, 1840, and on the 23d, assisted in laying out the foundations for old No. 1 furnace; and work upon it commenced in October following It was 35 feet high, and had an 8 ft. bosh.

I have the first bill of Mr. Samuel Slocum for boarding the workmen from Sept. 8, to Nov. 16, 1840. Mr. Manness states that the price was then $1.50 per week, including washing, and as the bill charges each person with the number of meals eaten, it is evident that 21 meals constituted a week's board. Common laborers' wages were then $17 per month. Carpenters seventy-five cents per day, all boarding themselves or paying for it.

1841   Thomas P. Harper came in the spring of 1841 and built the furnace water wheel.

Mr. C. F. Mattes had been here on a visit in 1840 but came to reside April 30, 1841, and has since had personal experience in almost every branch of the business of the Company.

Mr. George W. Scranton, who had been here quite frequently from the commencement of the iron works, commenced spending nearly all of his time here during the summer of 1841.

As near as can now be learned, Mr. Wm.

Henry left the iron works during the spring of 1842, and Mr. Scranton continued here, leaving his family in Belvidere, N. J., until succeeded by his brother, Selden T., in 1844, when the former moved to Oxford Furnace and took his brother Selden's place in charge of their business there. Mr. Samuel Templin made the first effort to blow in the furnace in September, 1841, and another later in the year, both being unsuccessful.

The following account is copied from a journal kept at the time: "*January 3, 1842.* Last night, at about eleven o'clock, the blast was put on the furnace under the superintendence of Mr. Henry, assisted by a Mr. Clarke, from Stanhope, N. J. At about three o'clock the furnace was bridged over the hearth. *January 4.* Hiram and Henry Johnson and Radle trying to work the furnace, but, finding it too hard, the boshes above the temp were removed and the coal and ore let slide through. *January 6.* H. and H. Johnson and Williams digging salamander out of the furnace."

1842

Three failures in succession to commence with, were enough to discourage the most sanguine. But these young pioneers must succeed, or financial ruin stared them in the face. After short naps in their straw bunks, improvised in the casting house, and having their meals brought to them, they went to work getting ready for another effort.

Mr. Selden T. Scranton, who was here to see the furnace put in operation, started for Danville to find, if possible, some one who had had some experience with making iron with anthracite fuel, and returned on January 10, 1842, bringing with him the late John F. Davis.

The necessary repairs having been made, blast was put on the furnace on the 18th, "blowing about two weeks without making any iron of consequence. After that the furnace began to work fairly and the blast was continued until February 26, when we blew out in consequence of our heating oven being insufficient—making iron, tons 75, 10 cwt."

"After putting in a new hearth and building two new heating ovens, in addition to altering the old one, we commenced the blast on the 23d May, 1842, and continued until 25th September (18 weeks), when we were obliged to blow out in consequence of the blowing apparatus giving way, being constructed too light in the beginning—making, iron 362 and castings about 12 tons; in all 374 tons.

1843   "After repairing bellows (wood blowing cylinders), putting in new pistons, &c., we commenced the blast on the 11th October (5 o'clock P. M.), and continued until March 12, 1843 (22 weeks), when we were obliged to blow out for want of limestone —making iron T, 583 tons 10 cwt., and castings about 17 tons; average per week 27 6.22 tons."

The quotations of these three successful blasts are from a paper by J. W. Sands, the bookkeeper of the firm.

Looking back from the present condition of the iron and steel business to the early struggles of the Lackawanna Iron Works, the whole operation appears insignificant. But it was a grand success, and enhanced by the fact that it followed three failures. It was a time of great anxiety with the proprietors, as shown by their desire to have their success known in a practical way—not waiting for the iron to cool before a pig of it was started by wagon for New Jersey by Mr. S. T. Scranton, as evidence of their success in making it with hard coal.

Mr. George Crane, of South Wales, states that he began the use of anthracite, with hot blast, on February 7, 1838, in a cupola blast furnace 41 ft. high, 10½ ft. across the boshes; product, 34 to 36 tons per week.

The first success in smelting iron ore in this country with anthracite was with a small experimental furnace built in 1838 at Weigh Lock, below Mauch Chunk; hight 21½ ft.; diameter of boshes, 5½ ft.; hearth, 19 by 21 inches. This furnace made, from July to November, 1839, during three months, two tons per day of Numbers 1, 2 and 3 grades; "fuel, anthracite exclusively."

"In the year 1840 there were only six furnaces using anthracite, two of them on the Schuylkill, three on the Susquehanna and one on the Lehigh, making 30 to 50 tons each."*

Having now demonstrated that iron could be made here with anthracite coal, the question to be settled was, could it be done and compete in the market with other furnaces. The ore used was partly a carbonate, mined about half way between the furnace and where the the old rolling mill is located, and the remainder at Briar Brook, some three miles distant on the Moosic mountain, and hauled in by teams that could bring but two loads per day; the carbonate averaging about 50 per cent., and the mountain ore little if any above 25 per cent. of iron. In December, 1840, to secure the iron ore thereon, 3,750 acres of mountain land was purchased of the Bank of North America for $11,250.

The only way to market at that time, and for years later, was to haul the iron by teams to Carbondale and ship by the Delaware and Hudson Canal Company's railroad to Honesdale, and thence by canal to New York, or cart it to Port Barnum, some eight miles, and ship it via the North Branch canal to Philadelphia or Baltimore. It was soon found that so crude a material could not bear such an expensive transportation and compete with other furnaces located nearer the market.

The natural conclusion was that something must be done to increase the value of the crude article, so that it would bear the expense of transportation, and the first thing necessary was more capital.

An effort was made which resulted in the formation of the limited partnership of Scrantons & Grant, September 3, 1843, with the capital increased from $20,000 to $86,000. Messrs. George W. and Selden T. Scranton and Sanford Grant being the general partners, and Philip H. Mattes, of Easton, Erastus C. and Joseph H. Scranton, of Augusta, Ga., and John Howland, of New York, the special partners.

In May, 1844, Mr. Manness contracted with 1844 the new firm to build the first rolling mill—110 ft. by 114 ft.—for the sum of $350; the firm agreeing to furnish all materials, including timber standing in the forests. The following November he

commenced building a nail factory, 50 ft. by 75 ft.
1845 The first iron was puddled in April, 1845, and the
first nails were made on the following 6th of July.
This year Mr. Joseph H. Scranton, during his
annual visit North, spent some time at the works
in September, when he purchased Mr. Grant's interest in the concern, on condition that Mr. Grant
should continue his services in the store until
April 1, 1846.

Mr. Scranton then visited Connecticut before
going south, and his accounts induced me to visit
"Lackawanna" in November, when I decided to
take an interest in the iron works and make this
my residence for ten years.

On my way here I obtained my first sight of a
telegraph line—the first line (consisting of two
wires only,) between New York and Philadelphia,—
which had been put up the summer or autumn
previous.

A Trip from New York to Scranton in 1846.

In order to show the saving of time in travel
during the last forty years, I propose to give an
account of our trip in March, 1846, when I
brought my small family here to reside.

There being no railroad, we came by the night
steamer from New Haven, and arriving in New

York the next morning, found the streets so full of snow that our carriage could hardly get to the Franklin House, on Broadway, corner of Dey street. After breakfast it was found impossible to get a hack to take us to the ferry, at the foot of Cortlandt street, on account of the depth of snow, consequently we had to walk, and a hand cart took our baggage. At that time the Morris and Essex railroad only ran between Newark and Morristown. Our car was hauled by the Camden and Amboy company over its road to Newark, where it was disconnected and drawn by four horses up the same heavy grade that is now used for steam. From this point we were taken by a locomotive with one pair of driving wheels to Morristown. At Summit Station we found a novel plan for supplying the engine with water. A pair of wheels on a line of shafting were placed beneath the track, the upper side of them being in line and level with its top. The locomotive was chained with its drivers resting on the wheels beneath the track, when the engineer put on steam and pumped what water he needed. At Morristown we took a stage and arrived at Oxford about dark. Here we spent about a week, owing partly to a heavy rain, which had so raised the Delaware river that we had to cross it by the bridge at Belvidere, and struck the river again at what is now Portland. We were

delayed in the Water Gap by ice and logs in the
road. After covering small bridges with slabs,
hauled out of the river, we finally reached Tan-
nersville, and spent the night. The next morning, finding good sleighing at Forks, we changed
our vehicle to runners, and again for wheels at
Greenville—now Nay-Aug—and arrived at Mr. S.
T. Scranton's about dark, March 17, 1846, the
traveling time being one day from New York to
Oxford, and two more to reach here. At present
the trip is made over substantially the same route
in 4½ hours, and from New Haven in 8 hours
frequently. This route generally took two days
and a half to or from New York, and was the usual
one followed. The only way to shorten the time
was to take the stage at Hyde Park at noon, and,
riding through the night, reach Middletown, N.
Y., in the afternoon ; then take the Erie railroad
to Piermont, and steamer down the Hudson, arriving in New York about 6 P. M. the next day
after leaving home. As the Erie road was extended to Otisville, Port Jervis and Narrowsburg,
the time was shortened, and in 1851, when the
road was opened to Binghamton and the Lackawanna and Western to Great Bend, we could reach
New York in twelve hours.

1846   April 1, 1846, Mr. Sanford Grant retired from
the concern, and the writer took his place in charge

of the store and as general purchaser for the concern, and later as real estate agent.

During his residence in Georgia, Mr. J. H. Scranton made the acquaintance of Mr. Fay, of the firm of Paddeford & Fay, of Savannah, Georgia, but formerly of Boston, Massachusetts. Hearing Mr. Scranton's reports of the immense deposits of coal; the comparative nearness to New York city; the success of making iron with anthracite, and other advantages of the location, this gentleman became quite interested in the iron works here, and thought that his eastern friends, being already in the manufacturing business, would very likely be glad to take a pecuniary interest in the works here. He therefore gave Mr. S. letters of introduction to his friends in Massachusetts, and wrote them that Mr. Scranton would call upon them and explain his plans.

In the meantime Mr. Selden T. Scranton had been corresponding with Messrs. Eno & Phelps, the latter being a director in the N. Y. & Erie R. R. Co., in reference to supplying that company with rails, and its making the concern a loan of $50,000 to erect the plant for that purpose. The result was a contract for 4,000 tons at $80 per ton, delivered at the rolling mill, but the railroad company had use, in building its road, for all the money it could raise and none to lend.

As usual, Mr. J. H. Scranton came north in the summer of 1846, when he accompanied Colonel George W. Scranton to this place.   After a general consultation, they left September 10, and spent the next week in New York, where they had interviews with Messrs. William E. Dodge, John J. Phelps and others.   They also met Messrs. Paddeford and Fay there, and then went to Boston, where they received a very cordial reception, and found many desirous of taking an interest in the iron works.   Mr. J. H. Scranton wrote from there on the 23d: "We were offered a cash advance of $100,000 if we could get clear of the contract with the Erie company, and would make one of the same character for 6,000 tons with as good a company as there is in New England."

The Messrs. Scranton having agreed to see the New York gentlemen before committing themselves to the Bostonians, returned to New York, where Mr. Dodge invited a number of his friends to meet them, and Messrs. William E. Dodge and Benjamin Loder, President of the N. Y. & Erie railroad, were appointed a committee to visit "Lackawanna" and report.   October 4th, Col. Scranton wrote from New York that Messrs. Loder and Dodge would leave for "Lackawanna" on the 15th.

The gentlemen arrived in due time, and al-

though there was a weekly paper published at
Providence, the ubiquitous reporter was not around,
and they supposed no one outside of the firm of
Scrantons & Platt would know them or suspect
their errand. They had not been here twenty-
four hours before Mr. Loder met an old schoolmate
in the redoubtable anti-corporation lawyer, Charles
Silkman, and privacy was abandoned. The gentlemen remained some two or three days and were
shown through the different departments of the
iron works, including the iron mines on the mountain, the coal mines in the valley, and the outcrop-
ping of coal at a number of places, that they might
judge for themselves as to its evident bountiful
supply.

On the 7th of November, 1846, the first firm of
Scrantons & Platt was duly organized upon the
basis of October 1, to take effect November 15.
With the retirement of Mr. Grant and change of
firm name to Scrantons & Platt, the following gen-
tlemen composed the partners in the firm: Messrs.
George W., Joseph H. and Selden T. Scranton,
and Joseph C. Platt, as general partners, and
Messrs. Philip H. Mattes, Edward Mowry and John
Howland, as special partners, with an additional
capital of $29,000, making the total $115,000.
Four days later—November 11—Messrs. William
E. Dodge, Anson G. Phelps, Benjamin Loder,

Samuel Marsh, Henry Shelden, John I. Blair, James Blair, William B. Skidmore, James Stokes, Philip Dater, Daniel S. Miller, John A. Robinson, William Henry Shelden and Frederick Griffing, put in another $115,000 as special partners.

1847   On October 2, 1847, some of the specials added to their subscriptions enough to make the capital $250,000.

During the winter of 1846-7 an additional contract for 8,000 tons of rails was made with the Erie company, on a sliding scale as to price, deliv- at the mouth of the Lackawaxen river, governed by the market, but within a maximum of $75 and a minimum of $65. Nearly the whole of the two contracts were filled. Soon after this an additional contract for 8,000 tons rails was made with the Erie Railroad company, on a sliding scale, to be governed by the market prices within a maximum of $85 and a minimum of $75.

As has been stated, Mr. Joseph H. Scranton had spent a part of the summers here since 1843. In June, 1847, he brought his family with him to make this his permanent residence. He came none too soon, for business was crowding and help needed.

The contracts with the Erie company made it necessary to enlarge the rolling mill and erect special machinery, which was so far accomplished that on the 23d of the next month (July) the first steam engine between Carbondale and Wilkes-Barre was started in it, and two rails made. On the 9th of August the mill commenced turning out rails regularly for the Erie company, which from that date were shipped in every way possible. The roads in all directions leading towards the railroad were full of teams hauling rails or returning empty, some days over seventy loads being sent off. All available teams were employed, and as some drivers took more rails than their teams could haul through, a portion was unloaded by the roadside, and could be seen by travelers for months after the last rail on the contract was delivered from the mill. As late as November, 1850, men were sent to pick up and forward them. On June 25, 1850, and from that date on, large numbers of rails were sent over our ore mine railroad to its junction with the Pennsylvania Coal Company's gravity road, and thence to the Delaware and Hudson Canal and distributed at points nearest the Erie railroad.

At the opening of the Lackawanna and Western railroad, in October, 1851, Mr. Benjamin Loder, President of the Erie railroad, was one of the guests, and in his remarks to the assemblage stated that, owing to the location of the iron works and the energy of its proprietors, the New York and Erie company had not only secured the release from the State of New York of all claim to a loan of $3,000,000, but had saved his company from bankruptcy, the Legislature of New York having offered to release all claim to the loan on condition that the road should be opened to Binghamton on or before a certain date, which was accomplished.

1848   Having but one blast furnace, and that a small one, it could not supply the rolling mill with the iron needed. A contract with Messrs. Quick & Moore was made for the erection of two, and during the winter the work was commenced. On July 23, 1848, Nos. 2 and 3 stone stacks were finished. No. 2 was first lighted Monday, September 24, 1849, and blast put on October 5. Blast was first put on No. 3, in November, 1849.

It appears to be inherent to all manufacturing business in this country, that every concern must be constantly making improvements to reduce the cost, and improve the article manufactured, in order to meet competition or lose its business. Such was the case with the Lackawanna Iron Works, and consequently more capital was needed, as before.

Col. G. W. Scranton and family, moved from Oxford to Scranton, June 21, 1848.

A second re-organization of the firm of Scrantons & Platt was arranged, more capital put in by new associates, and on November 1, 1848, the papers were signed, the capital being then $400,000.

THE LACKAWANNA IRON AND COAL COMPANY.

During the session of the Legislature for 1853, a special charter was granted to Scrantons & Platt and their associates, under which, on the 10th of March, 1853, The Lackawanna Iron & Coal Co. was organized, more money having been paid in and the capital increased from $400,000 to $800,000. The original stockholders were as follows : James Blair, John I. Blair, Philip Dater, William E. Dodge, F. R. Griffin's estate, Lucius Hotchkiss, John Howland, Benjamin Loder, Samuel Marsh, P. H. Mattes, D. S. Miller, Edward Mowry, Anson G. Phelps, J. C. Platt, John A. Robinson, Henry Sheldon, W. H. Sheldon, E. C. Scranton, G. W. Scranton, J. H. Scranton, S. T. Scranton, W. B. Skidmore, James Stokes ; total 8,000 shares. Mr. John Howland was by far the largest stockholder. Moses Taylor was probably interested in the company at the time of its organization, but does not appear as a stockholder until June 27, 1853. The following became stockholders in the order named : Theodore Sturges, 1856; Percy R. Pyne, 1861;

Samuel Sloan, 1864; William E. Dodge, jr., 1864; E. F. Hatfield, 1872 and B. G. Clarke, 1873. Mr. S. T. Scranton was made president of the company and remained so until he returned to Oxford in 1858, when he was succeeded by Joseph H. Scranton, who held the position until his death, June 6, 1872.

The business of the company continuing to increase, made still more capital necessary. The stockholders were again called upon, and the capital increased April 30, 1860, to $1,200,000, and again in 1873-4, when the steel works were built, $1,800,000 additional was put in by the stockholders, making the capital what it now is, $3,000,000.

ORE MINE RAILROAD.

The railroad to the ore mines on the mountain when built, was considered quite an enterprise. By act of the Legislature in March, 1848, Scrantons & Platt and their associates were authorized to build it. Mr. Seymour, of what has since been called Jessup, surveyed and located the road the same spring. Mr. H. H. Easton, from Syracuse, N. Y., was the builder—up to August 1, $15,000 had been expended upon it. On the line of this road a vein of limestone was discovered—some-

what of the oolitic order, the grains ranging about
the size of the end of one's little finger. It was
hoped it would answer for furnace purposes. On
December 1, a few car loads were brought down on
the new railroad for that purpose, and the transportation continued until it was found useless,
owing to the large admixture of rock with it. The
road was so far finished June 7, 1849, that a car
load of ore was run down to the furnace. The
cars were hauled to the mines—some five (5)
miles—by mules and run back by gravity. During this month a party of ladies and gentlemen
visited the mines, being one hour going out and
thirty-five minutes returning by loaded cars—the
speed being as fast as any of the party desired in
such cars.

RAILROADS.

(See page 12 for first project.)

The year 1849 witnessed the beginning of what, 1849
proved to be developments of great importance,
not only to Scranton, but to the entire coal basin
and its surroundings. Those interested in the
iron works soon found it was necessary to have a
more direct, expeditious and economical outlet to
market for their products. The demand for an

thracite coal was constantly increasing. The New
York and Erie Railroad was pushing its way to
Dunkirk on Lake Erie. All these things taken
into consideration, it was believed that with only
forty-eight miles of railroad to connect with the
Erie at Great Bend, coal could be delivered in
western New York markets at paying prices that
would defy competition. To insure business for
the railroad, it was proposed to purchase coal prop-
erties and open mines, to be operated by the company; and, as Col. Scranton put it, "Have a depot
full of freight all the time, waiting to be taken
away." The attention of capitalists was called to
the project, and sundry parties were brought here
to see for themselves the great abundance of coal,
and the business the iron works would give the
road; to which the almost universal reply was,
that they would want an interest in the iron works
also. This was so general that it was found necessary to accept the proposition in order to secure
the subscriptions necessary to build the railroad.
Subscriptions were then taken with the agreement
that they were to carry a pro rata interest in the
iron works, which the associates were to surrender
for the same amount in railroad stock. It was on
this basis that the firm of Scrantons & Platt built
the road and turned it over to the proper officers
in running order, without letting a contract for a

section on the entire line; Col. Scranton having
general supervision, assisted by Mr. Peter Jones,
of New Hampshire. I remember purchasing the
shovels, steel, sledges and other tools, besides hun-
dreds of barrels of beef and other provisions, which
Superintendent W. F. Hallstead and many others
delivered on the line "where they would do the
most good." This quotation recalls to mind the
fact that the shovels were made by O. Ames &
Sons, who stamped "Scrantons & Platt" in the
metal of each one, and the remains of them were
found along the line of the road for years later.

After considerable preparatory work for the
purpose, on March 7, 1849, Messrs. Henry W.
Drinker and Jeremiah Clark, as Commissioners,
held a meeting at the hotel kept by D. K. Kressler
and opened books for subscriptions for stock of the
Liggett's Gap Railroad.* Over $250,000 were re-
ceived, and ten per cent. on the amount paid in.

The day had passed for operating railroads by
horse power, and providing, under $20 fine, that the
conductor of a wagon should blow a horn to notify
the collector to be ready to take toll, consequently
Mr. S. T. Scranton started for Harrisburg on the
9th (via New York and Philadelphia, as the

---

*On the northwest end of the Washington Avenue car shops
can still be seen two keystones of iron, bearing the letters "L.
G. R. R. S., 1851."

quickest route), and was successful in getting
legislation enabling the company to operate the
road with locomotives, and make such other
changes necessary to make the enterprise a success.

PRELIMINARY SURVEY.

April 25, 1849, Mr. James Seymour, of Seymour, since called Jessup, under the general direction of Major Morrell, of New York, commenced
the preliminary survey for the Liggett's Gap Railroad.

The following is copied from the original minutes now in my possession:

" Pursuant to public notice, a meeting of the
stockholders in the Liggett's Gap Railroad Co.
was held at the house of D. K. Kressler, in the
village of Harrison, Luzerne county, Pa., at 2
o'clock, on the afternoon of Wednesday, January
2, 1850.

" The meeting was organized by the appointment of Henry W. Drinker, chairman, and John
Sherrerd, secretary.

" On motion of H. W. Drinker, Esq., the meeting proceeded to the election of officers and managers of the company for the present year, or until
others are elected to fill their places.

"On motion of H. W. Drinker, Esq., it was re-solved that the Board of Managers be requested to appoint a committee to facilitate the business of the company.

"William H. Tripp and Joseph C. Platt were appointed judges of election.

"On motion the polls were closed at 4:30 o'clock, P. M.

"On an inspection of the votes, the following named gentlemen were declared duly elected to their respective offices, each having received 633 votes, being the whole number polled, representing twenty-nine hundred and sixty-six shares of stock.

"Officers: John J. Phelps, President; Selden T. Scranton, Treasurer; Charles F. Mattes, Secretary.

"Managers: John I. Blair, Frederick R. Griffing, Daniel S. Miller, Henry W. Drinker, Jeremiah Clark, Joseph H. Scranton, Joseph C. Platt, Andrew Bedford, George W. Scranton and Charles Fuller.

"On motion it was resolved that the Board of Managers do now organize a meeting of that body.

"HENRY W. DRINKER, Chairman.

"Attest: JOHN S. SHERRERD, Secretary."

April 30, 1850, Mr. Peter Jones arrived bringing his men and the implements he had used in re-building the Cayuga & Susquehanna Railroad   1850

from Owego to Ithaca—for the Liggett's Gap interest—which was to connect the Erie R. R. with the
Erie Canal, via Cayuga Lake, for the transportation of Scranton coal.   The grading of the Liggett's Gap Railroad was commenced early in May,
but before the month closed there was an Irish
war in Liggett's Gap between the "Corkonians"
and "Far-downers," as they called each other.

IRISH WAR—MAY, 1850.

Each side was determined to drive the other
off the road, but both parties were, if possible,
more hostile to the Germans, and as determined
to oust them.   The Germans armed themselves
and continued at their work.   A battle was fought
on the 28th, one person being killed instantly and
a number wounded, all of whom were said to be
"Corkonians."   Two bodies were found in the
woods near by the following month, bearing marks
of having been shot.   On the 30th the Connaught
men, to the number of some 200, returned to drive
the "Corkonians" further.   On their way they
came to the "Dutch Shanty" and demanded the
fire-arms, but failed to get them.   The Irish were
said to be armed with almost everything that
could be used in a melee, including guns, pistols,

stones, sticks—one had an iron candlestick and another part of a buck-saw fastened to a shovel handle. Neither party succeeded in driving off the other. Work was soon resumed.

During the Legislative session of 1851, author- 1851 ity was given to change the name from "Liggett's Gap" to the "Lackawanna and Western Railroad Company," and the change was made on the 14th of the following April.

The first locomotive bought for the road was the "Pioneer," from the Cayuga and Susquehanna railroad. It came down the river on an ark from Owego to near Pittston. The first one set in operation on the road was the "Spitfire." It was of English make and bought of the Reading Railroad company, by Mr. D. S. Dotterer, who took some pride in getting his purchase on the road first. Both engines came from Port Griffith, on the Pennsylvania Coal Company's railroad to the junction of the ore mine railroad, and by the latter to the iron rolling mill. Mr. Dotterer ran the "Spitfire" its first trip from the rolling mill on Friday, May 16, 1851. It being the first locomotive that many here had seen, it was a great curiosity, and when it reached the furnaces was covered by men and boys, some of them astride of it. The first engine that came down on the road from Great Bend was the "Wyoming," on the 11th of October, 1851, having two passenger cars.

On the opening day, October 15, 1851, sixty-five ladies and gentlemen, the latter being nearly all interested in the railroad and iron works, came over the railroad from Great Bend to Scranton in 2¾ hours. On the next day the first coal train was started for Ithaca, N. Y. October 20, a passenger train commenced regular trips, with Mr. R. W. Olmstead as temporary conductor.

On the 22d I made my first all rail trip to New York, returning on the 29th, leaving there at 6 A. M. and reaching home at 6 P. M., duly appreciating the great improvement over staging to Narrowsburg to reach the Erie railroad, or the earlier and longer trips I had made so many times.

That a railroad to Great Bend was only a part of the improvements contemplated by the associates interested in the iron works, will be readily admitted when attention is called to the fact that before the road to Great Bend was opened, on October 15, 1851, a meeting had been held at the house of Jacob Knecht, in Stroudsburg, November 28, 1850, by the commissioners authorized to receive subscriptions to the capital stock of the Delaware and Cobb's Gap railroad. Eighteen thousand shares of $50 each were subscribed for by the following gentlemen: John I. Blair, T. W. Gale, J. H.

Scranton, J. C. Platt, Scrantons & Platt, F. R. Griffing, Samuel Marsh, Edward Mowry, William E. Dodge, John J. Phelps, James Stokes, Daniel S. Miller, J. S. Sturges, Roswell Sprague, Henry Hotchkiss, George Bulkley, Anson G. Phelps, each 1,000 shares; S. T. Scranton, 480; George W. Scranton, 500; James M. Porter, Samuel Taylor, Philip H. Mattes, and H. W. Nicholson, each 5 shares; on which ten per cent., or $90,000, was paid in. A meeting of the subscribers or stockholders was held in Stroudsburg, December 26, 1850, when the following officers were elected:

Officers—George W. Scranton, President; John I. Blair, Treasurer; Charles F. Mattes, Secretary.

Directors—John J. Phelps, William E. Dodge, T. W. Gale, L. L. Sturges, John I. Blair, S. T. Scranton, J. H. Scranton, J. C. Platt, H. W. Nicholson, James M. Porter, James H. Stroud, and Franklin Starbourne.

Mr. John S. Sherrerd wrote in diary: "On April 8, 1851, Mr. E. McNeil commenced an exploration survey for Cobb Gap and Delaware railroad."

March 11, 1853, the Delaware and Cobb's Gap 1853 was merged with the Lackawanna and Western, under the name of Delaware, Lackawanna and Western Railroad Company. May 27, 1854, the 1854 first anthracite coal burning locomotive was put on the road.

The passenger depot for the Lackawanna and Western railroad was located in the rear of the west corner of Lackawanna and Wyoming Avenues, fronting on Wyoming Avenue, and the freight depot fronted on Washington in rear of west corner of Lackawanna and Washington Avenues. In order to get a desirable grade and location for the road to be continued southerly towards New York, both depots had to be moved to and near the present location of the passenger depot, opposite Franklin Avenue. This removal was commenced February 17, 1854, by D. H. Dotterer, superintendent. They were wooden buildings, and afterwards were annexed for an enlarged freight depot, when Superintendent Watts Cooke erected the brick depot which later has been enlarged and very much improved.

1855   January 8, 1855, the track-layers on the Southern Division crossed the upper end of Lackawanna Avenue, and on May 10, following, the first locomotive ran through the tunnel near the falls of Roaring Brook.

There having been some disagreement between the railroad company officials and Malone & Co., contractors, as to the amount due, the latter (Malone & Co.), on June 5, 1855, armed some of their men and placed them on guard to prevent the company's men laying rails on their section, near No. 6 dam of the Pennsylvania Coal Company. The railroad officials tried mild methods until August 21, when a train of platform cars, loaded with men well armed, having on the forward car the old cannon " Sam " mounted on a swivel, and charged with missiles, such as old spikes, was sent up the road. On arriving at the disputed territory, President George D. Phelps told the Malones that he should take possession of the road-bed, and preferred to do it peacefully. After considerable talk, including some high words, the contractors gave possession. The obstructions were removed, possession maintained, and in the afternoon track-laying commenced. From this time there was nothing to prevent the prosecution of work on the road, so that on May 15, 1856, a single passenger 1856 car commenced regular trips to Delaware station, from which place stages ran to Belvidere—some three miles—from whence there was then railroad connections, as now, to New York *via* New Jersey Central from Phillipsburg, and Philadelphia *via* Trenton. On the 27th of the same month the Southern Division was formally opened by an excursion of the officers and proprietors and their friends, from New York by the Central Railroad of New Jersey to the junction near New Hampton, and thence to Scranton.

This was a proud day for Scranton. Direct communication by rail of only 146 miles from the metropolis of the nation, through to the northwest as far as any of the larger towns of the country possessed such advantages. Time has shown that the enterprise as a whole was not only a wise one, but was undertaken none too soon for the benefit of the entire northern coal basin.

On the day following—May 28—a number of Scrantonians accompanied the excursionists on their return as far as Greenville—now Nay-Aug— where our party from Scranton were invited by the late Hon. William Jessup, President, to open his railroad (the " Lackawanna ") to Jessup, which we did, and returned the same way.

June 9, 1856, a regular passenger train commenced running to Clarksville (until a passenger station could be built at the Junction). A change was here made to the Central of New Jersey, which at that time ran to Elizabethport, where connection with New York was made by steamboat, *via* Kill von Kull, to Pier No. 2 North River. At a later period passengers were taken for awhile *via* Elizabeth, Newark and Jersey City to the foot of Cortlandt Street. Still later *via* the extension of the New Jersey Central across the mouth of Newark Bay to Communipaw and Liberty Street, and finally, as at present, *via* the Morris and Essex railroad to Hoboken and Barclay or Christopher Streets in New York.

TOWN PLOT.

When Mr. Henry named the place Harrison (about the time of the Harrison campaign in 1841), he made a " Plan of Harrison, Providence township, Luzerne county, by William Henry," which I now hold. The following are the names of the streets on it: "Lackawanna," "George," "Selden," "Sanford," "Philip," "William," "Mary," and "Mott," the second and third being evidently intended for the Messrs. Scranton, the next for Mr. Grant, followed by "Philip" H. Mattes, "William" and "Mary" Henry, and lastly Barton "Mott." None of these streets were regularly opened for travel except "William," which was the old emigrant road from Dunmore to Pittston *via* the bridge over Roaring Brook at the brick grain mill. This road was vacated some years since by the court of Luzerne county, from the top of the hill (northerly from the bridge), where the first school house formerly stood, to the intersection of Quincy Avenue and Gibson Street. None of these names except

Lackawanna have been perpetuated on the plot of Scranton; and it will be noticed that not a name of any officer or stockholder of the property has been used in naming the avenues or streets. The city officials have lately used the names of some of our citizens in connection with the alleys—a questionable compliment.

In 1850, when the first steps were taken to lay out the village plot, I felt it a matter of importance to start right, and held many consultations with Mr. Joel Amsden, the engineer. Mr. Amsden, appreciating the interest evinced, probably consulted me more than the other partners of the firm; consequently, being better informed in the details, the lot business naturally devolved upon me, and I had charge of it for Scrantons & Platt until the dissolution of the firm. To Mr. Amsden is due the credit of the plan of door yards which is so universally popular, and which a number are disposed to abuse by putting small shops thereon, which they have no right to do. Mr. Amsden made three sketches or plots for selection, and was instructed to adopt the one best suited to extend the plot up and down the valley, regardless of the side lines of the tracts belonging to the firm.

As soon as the plot was decided upon, steps were taken to build a hotel, as an absolute neces-

sity, if it was expected to have travelers entertained;
Mr. Kressler's hotel, which he named the "Scranton House," being always full without them.
Notwithstanding some wag envious of Scranton's
enterprise, nicknamed the Wyoming House the
" Scranton Folly," time has shown it to have been
good policy. It was not built for making money,
or as a speculation, but to have a hotel that would
be a credit to the place and help build it up. The
building and furnishing, exclusive of the lots, cost
about $40,000. It was sold to Mr. J. C. Burgess
after he had run it a few years for $37,500. His
first guests (three ladies and two gentlemen) were
entertained July 12, 1852, but the regular opening
of the hotel was a few days later.

On the organization of the Lackawanna Iron
and Coal Company—June 10, 1853—I was made
officially Real Estate Agent and Store-keeper.
On the death of Mr. J. H. Scranton, being made
Vice-President of the Company, I continued at-
tending to the real estate business until my resignation, December 31, 1874. Thus having charge
of the village plot and extensions made from time
to time, it devolved upon me to name a large pro-
portion of the streets. Therefore, upon the suggestion of one of our citizens, the history of the
selection of names for some of the avenues and
streets is here given: Lackawanna and Wyo-

ming Avenues are the widest streets we have—
each being 100 ft. between the building lines and
60 ft. between the curb stones, the others being
generally 80 ft. and 40 ft. The former was intended—as it has proved to be—the main business
thoroughfare. Both were named in compliment
to the two valleys by general consultation.
What is now Washington Avenue it was first proposed to call Church Street. Mr. Selden T. Scranton proposed that it should be called Washington
Avenue, which was at once adopted, and the plan
to call all streets running parallel with it on the
northerly side of Roaring Brook, avenues. Penn
and Franklin having been named after the noted
Pennsylvanians, the name of the first Governor
of the State—Mifflin—was given to the remaining
avenue on that side of the plot; and then of the
Presidents in succession, including the younger
Adams in the name of Quincy. Afterwards the
name of Jackson Avenue was given to a street in
Petersburg in line with one of ours, and by request
the name was continued on the plot of Scrantons
& Platt. Pittston Avenue was so named thinking
that probably a bridge would be built across Roaring Brook near the furnaces, and thus connect it
with Lackawanna Avenue and make it the main
thoroughfare to Pittston, and avoid the hills by
the old route *via* the brick grain mill and the

bridge, lower down Roaring Brook to Cedar Street.
Capouse Avenue was named for the chief of a tribe
of Indians, and Monsey Avenue for the tribe itself,
to perpetuate the aboriginal names of this locality.[*]
Webster, Clay, Irving, Prescott, Lincoln and Ban-
croft Avenues were named for those noted Ameri-
cans.

To Mr. Joel Amsden, the engineer of the plot,
we are indebted for the suggestion to use the
names of our trees for the streets. The particular
names were mostly selected and placed by me. I
well remember taking a sign marked "Beech
Street," and finding the only tree in line of it was
a birch, I had another painted to correspond
with the tree. On returning to put up the sign
the tree was gone, but the street retains the name
of Birch. Alder Street ran through a swamp of
alders—now filled with ashes from the rolling
mill and upon which quite a number of buildings
are erected. Hickory Street received its name
from a hickory tree on the flats in line with it.
River Street from its running parallel with the
Lackawanna river until that part was taken possession of by the Union railroad, now belonging
to and operated by the Delaware and Hudson

[*] "The Monsey or Munsey Indians, the wolf tribe of the Dela-
wares."—Pierce's History, page 217. "They had a famous chief
whose name was Capouse."—Page 221.

Canal company. Orchard Street started in the old orchard, three trees of which were standing when the street was laid out. Hemlock Street, from there being many of them in the neighborhood and hemlock shanties built of it. Moosic Street, on account of its being the most direct to that mountain. Cliff Street, for the reason that it crossed one. Anthony Street, from the fact that the writer had sold three of the four or five lots on the street to men of that name before naming it. Brook Street, because it crossed Pine brook. Bank Street was cut into a side hill or bank to make it. Ridge Row was so named by S. T. Scranton before the town plot was laid out, when Mr. J. H. Scranton built the frame dwelling on the ridge where he lived so long, and near where the stone mansion now stands, but the street was not opened until after the Southern Division of the D., L. & W. R. R. was built. It was mostly blasted out of solid rock from near the present front gate of Mrs. Scranton's residence to the westerly end of the wall in front of my own residence, and the material used to ballast the railroad track. Prospect Street, from its view of the village north of Roaring Brook. Stone Avenue will be found very appropriate, having been so named because it lies on a ridge of rocks. Vale Street, from having commenced in a vale (valley). Crown

Street started on the crown of the hill where it is located.

FIRST BOROUGH ELECTION AND ORGANIZATION AND CHARTER OF THE CITY.

At the first election of Scranton borough there 1856 were 371 votes polled. Joseph Slocum received 367 for Burgess.

Town Council—James Harrington, 245; J. C. Platt, 366; John Nincehalser, 366; David K. Kressler, 216; William Ward, 213.

Assessor—William P. Carling, 367.

Auditors—Joseph Chase, 243; Richard Drinker, 220; Henry L. Marion, 363.

Constable—James McKinney, 359.

School Directors—William P. Jenks, 218; John Grier, 219; G. W. Brock, 245; A. L. Horn, 219; C. E. Lathrop, 218.

Poor Directors—Charles Fuller, 348; David Kemmon, 233.

The borough was organized after the election by the above town council under a general law.

The city of Scranton, composed of three boroughs of Scranton, Providence and Hyde Park, was chartered in 1866.

NEWSPAPERS.

The first paper published between Carbondale and Wilkes-Barre was called the *The Country Mirror and Lackawannian*, a weekly. It had been published as the *Carbondale Gazette*; Mr. Frank B. Woodward brought it to Providence in 1845 or very early in 1846. The writer has a copy of its last issue of March 10, 1847, containing Mr. Woodward's valedictory, in which he states his intention to regain his health and spirits in tilling the soil with his venerable father. The editorial has a heading " Henry Clay Our First Choice and the Repeal of the British Tariff of 1846."

The first paper published in Scranton was the *Lackawanna Herald*, a weekly, by Mr. Charles E. Lathrop, now residing in Carbondale. The first number was issued March 1, 1853. He sold out in 1856 to E. B. Chase. Mr. Lathrop has a full file of the *Herald* for the time he published it.

A second importation from Carbondale was the *Spirit of the Valley*, a weekly. First number, January 25, 1855, by Messrs. J. B. Adams and T. J. Alleger, who continued its publication for a year or so. February 1, 1855, the first number of the *Tri-Weekly Experiment* was issued by F. Dilley.

In 1856 Mr. E. B. Chase purchased the *Lacka-*

wanna Herald and the *Spirit of the Valley.* He published them as the *Herald of the Union* until 1859, when he sold to Doctor Davis and J. B. Adams. The latter sold out to Doctor Wheeler.

In 1856 Mr. Theodore Smith came here from Montrose and commenced the publication of the *Scranton Republican.* In 1858 it was purchased by Mr. F. A. McCartney, who in 1863 sold it to Mr. Thomas F. Alleger. In March, 1866, Mr. F. A. Crandall purchased a half interest and finally became its sole proprietor. During this year Mr. Crandall sold a half interest to Mr. R. N. Eddy, of Cazenovia, N. Y. In September, 1867, Mr. J. A. Scranton purchased Mr. Eddy's interest, and on the 1st of November following, *The Morning Republic*, a daily, was published. In March, 1869, Mr. Scranton purchased the interest of Mr. Crandall and has continued the publication of both daily and weekly to this time.

CENSUSES.

The first census of this country was provided for by the Constitution and was taken in 1790. It gives enumerations of no territory less than counties. Luzerne county then included the greater part of Bradford, all of Susquehanna, Wyoming, and Lackawanna counties, the population being 4,904. The next was in 1800, when Providence—one of the seventeen townships of Luzerne—had a population of 579; in 1810, 589; 1820 (including one colored man), 861; 1830 (including one colored man, no aliens), 976; 1840 (including one colored man, no aliens), 1,169.

The era of the prosperity of Scranton and vicinity dates from this time, and undoubtedly was owing to the impetus given to business by the commencement of the iron business by Messrs. Scrantons, Grant & Co.—the details of which are given in the account of the Lackawanna Iron Works.

During the winter of 1847-8, a census was taken of the territory which afterwards became the borough of Scranton, giving the names of the heads of families and number of each sex, the object being to get a postoffice. Mr. O. P. Clark, postmaster of Hyde Park, certifies that seven-tenths of the mail received at his office came to Harrison—as the place was then called, or the Lackawanna Iron Works. This census shows there were then 205 families, 873 males and 523 females or 1,396, or 227 more than the whole township contained in 1840. The United States census for 1850 is:

Scranton, the same territory, ... 2,230
Providence borough 446
Providence township, including (4) colored . 4,467

Total for the township . . . . ⁚ . 7,143

In 1854 a census was taken by Mr. E. G. Cour- 1854
sen, assisted by Mr. Charles Fuller, both being
in the employ of the Lackawanna Iron and Coal
Co. This shows the names of heads of families,
occupation, nationality, and is summed up by Mr.
Fuller as follows:

Males, 2,478; Females, 1,768 .   . 4,241
  353 Irish   families .   . 1,795
  154 German   "   795
   81 Welsh   "   415
   16 English   "   85
  175 American   "   1,151

  779   4,241

Single men included 585—and he adds " should
be 800."

  Irish   servant girls .   .   . 49
  German   "   "   ⁚ 10
  American   "   "   2

Total 61

Of these the hotels employ 23. At the iron
ore mines on the mountains there were:

2 Welsh	families,	4 males,	4 females
2 Irish	"	7 "	9 "
14 American	"	47 "	32 "
		58	45—103

1860   The United States census for 1860 was:

Providence borough 1,410
   "   township 4,097
Hyde Park   "   . 3,360— 8,867
Scranton borough . 9,223

Total for the entire township   18,090

1870   In 1870, Scranton city (including Providence
        and Hyde Park boroughs) 35,092
Dunmore borough 4,311

Total for township 39,403

1880   In 1880, Scranton city 45,850
Dunmore borough 5,151

Total for township 51,001
An increase in 40 years of 49,832.

1886   The Directory of 1886, states : " The Census
and Directory for 1880 gave 4⅓ individuals to the
Directory names." The number of names in this
Directory approximates 20,000, which, computing
on the basis of 4⅓ persons to a name, would place
the population of Scranton at 86,666.

ODD FELLOWS' HALL.

The Odd Fellows' Hall played quite a conspic-
uous part in the early days of Scranton. It occupied a part of the triangle in front of the L. I. &
C. Co.'s offices, formed by the junction of Lackawanna and Jefferson Avenues and Ridge Row. It
stood on a ridge of rocks some fifteen feet above
the present grade of the streets. The second story
was used exclusively by societies of various kinds ;
the first for religious and other public exercises,
schools, &c., being the only public hall in the
place. It was built in 1847–8, and was taken
down in 1868 to make make room for the Lackawanna Iron and Coal Co.'s stores and offices, and
re-erected where it now stands—on the hill northerly from the old iron rolling mill, and converted
into four dwelling houses. The building was first
used March 1, 1848, by the Union Sunday school.
It was used by five societies of Odd Fellows, four
Temperance societies and three Masonic. The
First Presbyterian, Penn Avenue Baptist, St.
Luke's Episcopal, German Presbyterian and German Lutheran churches, all used it for worship,
and nearly, if not all, were organized in it. The
Universalists held four services in it. It was
also used by the Union, Welsh, and Presbyterian

Sunday schools, a number of beneficial societies, clubs, a brass band, lyceum, nine private schools, a union league, and lastly but not the least, for a United States military hospital, in charge of Capt. Mattison, October 26 to December 31, 1863. At the same time the building now belonging to Messrs. Clark & Snover was used as United States barracks.

Churches.

Rev. N. G. Parke, of Pittston, in his historical discourse of October, 25, 1879, says: "The Moravians must be regarded as the pioneer missionaries in this Susquehanna region. Count Zinzindorf, as early as 1742, while connected with the Moravian Mission in Bethlehem, visited the valley and preached along the Susquehanna and up the Lackawanna as far as Capouse meadows north of Scranton." He also states that, "after the resignation of the Rev. Ard Hoyt, in Wilkes-Barre, in 1817, the church was without a pastor until the settlement of the Rev. Cyrus Gildersleeve in 1821. Up to this time preaching in the Lackawanna valley had been only occasional. From the settlement of Mr. Gildersleeve over the church in Wilkes-Barre, preaching in the Lackawanna valley became stated and regular. He regarded it as part of his parish." - Mr. E. A. Atherton, our present Register of the county, states that in 1826-7, Mr. William Wood " was the junior pastor of the First Presbyterian church at Wilkes-Barre, while the Rev. Cyrus Gildersleeve was the senior. That the field occupied by the Wilkes-Barre church extended from Hanover on the south, Kingston and Northmoreland on the west, and Providence on the north. The congregations met in winter in private houses and in summer in barns. Many of the people came several miles in rude lumber wagons, sometimes drawn by oxen."

A description of one of the congregations as they were seated in a barn might not be amiss in these days of costly churches and splendid equipage. The preacher had a stand before him on which lay a Bible and hymn book, and a chair was behind him. Board seats arranged on the threshing floor were occupied by the older men and women including the children, while the younger men and boys mounted the first tier of girths with their feet dangling in mid-air, mostly without shoes. How would this suit the youngsters of the present day? Mr. Wood was aided in his labors by Mr. Zebulon Butler, a brother of the Hon. Chester Butler. Quoting again from Mr. Parke's discourse: "The people were poor and scattered and the religious societies only partially organized ;

still the tardiness of the early settlers in both valleys in moving to erect houses of worship is a no-
ticeable fact; this is especially true in Lackawanna
valley.   Assuming that the Baptists organized a
church here in 1776, they were for more than fifty
years without a sanctuary or a settled ministry;
and any preaching that was done by Congregationalists, up to 1820, was in school houses, barns
and private houses, and without charge to th .
people.   The old settlers were not 'Gospel har
ened,' for they did not have much of it; but so ;
as appears they did not care to build churches (
sustain the ministry.   This indifference had not
all subsided in 1840, when the foundations of
Scranton were laid, as those living can testify, nor
in 1844 when I was commissioned to labor her̃e a:
a missionary."

"Rev. John Dorrance, D. D., who in 1833 succeeded Doctor Nicholas Murray in the pastorate of
the Wilkes-Barre church, had labored in the Lackawanna valley while a theological student, in connection with Zebulon Butler, Thomas Janeway,
William Wood and others—he gave special attention to the Lackawanna field.   Unable himself to
keep up the meetings, he procured missionaries to
do the work.   Among those who labored in the
valley under his direction, previously to 1841,
were the Rev. Thomas Owen, Rev. John Turbot,

Rev. Owen Brown and Rev. William Tod. The
Rev. T. F. Hunt did good service for the cause of
Christ in this field, and largely at his own charges.
The labors of Mr. Hunt in the neighborhood of
Providence and Scranton, before there were any
sanctuaries for God in that region, are still bearing
fruit. The Rev. Charles Evans was the last missionary (Presbyterian) in the field previous to my
ming here. He left in the spring of 1844 to
ept a call from the church of Northmoreland."
As above stated, Mr. Parke was in 1844 commis-
ned as a missionary for the territory included
 the townships of Providence, Lackawanna and
Pittston, and did good service therein—preaching
his farewell sermon here June 17, 1849, and has
nce devoted himself to his church and congrega-
on at Pittston. Mr. Parke quotes the testimony
 an old settler, now over four score years old, as
o the character of the population of Lackawanna
valley during the first twenty years of its settlement. He says: " Notwithstanding the heteroge-
neous material of which this community was com-
osed, there was a strong religious element pervad-
ng the minds and the hearts of the whole community, making a law-abiding people, and present-
ing to the devoted missionary of the Cross an
ample field ready for harvesting." Hence the
early success of the Methodists under William

Butler and his successors. Elder John Miller, (a Baptist minister of Abington), as early as 1806, had made a lodgment in the valley, and had captured a goodly number of the old Congregationalists, and even some of the " new-fledged Methodists." So far as can be learned, the first church organization in the township of Providence—certainly in Scranton proper—was Presbyterian. Rev. N. G. Parke gives the records of Susquehanna Presbytery as authority, that on February 25, 1842, a Presbyterian church was organized " in the school house in the village of Harrison." This school house stood at the top of the hill near the present blast furnaces, and in the forks of the Providence and Dunmore roads as then used, and was first used in September, 1840, opening with seven scholars. Mr. J. W. Sands, one of the twenty-eight persons who joined in the organization, made the following entry in a journal he was keeping at that time : " Friday, 25th February, 1842, at 11:30 o'clock, a meeting commenced in the school house conducted by the Rev. Messrs. Dorrance, Hunt and Brown. At 2 o'clock a church was organized, to be under the direction or a branch of the Presbyterian church of the United States. Messrs. Couch and Atherton elected elders ; Mr. H. B. Daily, deacon." This was known as the " Lackawanna Presbyterian Church," and intended to cover the territory before stated. Mr. Parke's church at Pittston is a continuance of the same organization.

CHURCH EDIFICES.

An article in the *Scranton Republican* of May 18, 1884, states that the first church edifice in Hyde Park was Unitarian and stood on "Main Avenue" where Joseph A. Mears then resided, but gave no date of its erection. This edifice, and the Methodist or "Village Chapel" in Scranton—as it was called at first—were the only church edifices for some years after 1846, between Carbondale and Wilkes-Barre, except the old Baptist church in Blakely, now standing near the forks of the road leading to Peckville. The earliest record of this "Village Chapel" to be found, is on the books of Scranton, Grant & Co., July 23, 1841, when the following names were charged with subscriptions they had made and the chapel credited with the total amount:

William Henry . . .	. $10.00
Daniel Dodge .	3.50
S. W. Nolton	2.50
George Whitman	2.50
Jacon Gerstle	2.00˙

Henry R. Manness. . . . . . $ 2.00

Ferdinand Dulot .   . . 1.00

Caleb Robins 1.00

Patrick Hart. .   1.00

S. W. Colckglasser .   1.00

John Snyder.   .   .50

John L. Travis. .   .   .50

Simon Ward (September 3) .   1.00

Total. $28.50

August 10, 1853, Mr. William Henry wrote
Mr. Charles Fuller in reference to the " Village
Chapel": " We commenced in 1841 and finished it
early in 1842. While this house was to be under
the supervision of the Methodists of this vicinity,
other evangelical denominations were not excluded
from using it as a house of worship." This
" Chapel " stood on a lot 70x155, given by Scranton, Grant & Co., partly in what is now Adams
avenue at its junction with Lackawanna avenue on
a bluff some ten feet high, which has been removed in grading the avenues. The corner of the
" Chapel " was almost exactly where the corner of
Messrs. Jifkins meat market is, but not in line
with the avenue. The city plot was laid out in
1850–1, and in order that the two avenues named
could be opened where they are now, Scrantons &
Platt, in 1855–6, gave the three lots now occupied

by the Methodist church and parsonage near by, on Adams avenue, and two thousand dollars in building materials in exchange for the old lot one hundred feet front by one hundred and twelve deep. It being then impossible to move the "Chapel" through either Adams, Washington, Wyoming or Penn avenues owing to the swamp or Lily pond crossing them, the building was taken down August 20, 1856, and re-erected on the south corner of Adams avenue and Vine street, where it can now be seen on the alley on the rear of the lot. The only change in its exterior is that it has an octagon instead of a square cupola or tower. The "Chapel" was generally used on alternate Sabbaths by the Presbyterians and Methodists, the only real change being in the preachers and not in the audiences.

The second church edifice erected here was the Roman Catholic, a wooden building, situated on what is now the west corner of Stone and Hemlock streets. It was raised on Saturday, June 24, 1848.

The third church building here was the Welsh Calvinistic Methodist. It was a small wooden building, originally standing on the westerly end of Rome street in the old Slocum orchard, south of Roaring Brook. When the plot of 1850-1 was laid out this street was abolished, and later the

building was moved to front on River street.   The
lot it occupied here was purchased by the German
Catholics and is now occupied by the school connected with their church.   The building was purchased by the Baptists and moved to block 80 on
Pittston avenue.   This building was first used
March 18, 1849, and was dedicated July 8,
following.

The next organization in order of date is believed to be what is now the "First Presbyterian
Church of Scranton, Pa.," on Washington avenue.
Early in the summer of 1848 a meeting of those
interested in the Presbyterian form of worship was
held, of which Mr. Nathaniel B. Hutchison—formerly of Belvidere, New Jersey—was made chairman, and J. C. Platt, secretary.   At this meeting
the chairman and Mr. Charles Fuller, both ruling
elders in the churches to which they belonged,
were made a committee "to examine the charters
and by all other available means obtain knowledge
which enable the people to decide whether Lackawanna church is here or at Pittston."   "July 10,
1848, a meeting was held in the Odd Fellows' Hall,
of Presbyterians with their adherents, to hear the
report of the committee appointed to learn the
truth as the *locus ubi* of the church of Lackawanna.
A letter was read from the pastor at this meeting,
in which he stated his conviction that the Harrison,

Lackawanna and Pittston churches were all one, and that Harrison must be considered the head of the church although it was called Lackawanna. At this meeting, after 'deliberation and consultation,' as the record states, it was unanimously agreed that the interests of the church required a separate organization at this point. Mr. Charles Fuller was accordingly appointed as a committee to secure from the Presbytery such an organization, to be called the church of Harrison. Another committee was authorized to rent the Odd Fellows' Hall at $12 a year for purposes of worship. Of this meeting Joseph H. Scranton was secretary, and, as it would seem, was one of the chief actors."* The committee circulated a petition, and in due time, presented it to the Presbytery of Luzerne, asking for a church organization. This petition was signed by eighteen communicants and a number of citizens who proposed to identify themselves with the congregation, though not professing Christians. In answer to this petition, a committee of the Presbytery—consisting of Rev. John Dorrance, D. D. and Rev. N. G. Parke—called the people together on the 14th day of October, 1848, and, after a sermon by Mr. Dorrance, proceeded to the organization of a church according to the

---

* Dr. S. C. Logan's sermon, November 16, 1873.

order and discipline of the Presbyterian Confession. They received and enrolled in this organization seventeen persons—eight men and nine women. Its name was afterwards changed to the " First Presbyterian Church of Scranton, Pa." The Rev. J. Delville Mitchell first preached here August 18, 1848, and occasionally afterwards. Thursday evening, August 2, 1849, at a general meeting of the citizens, it was decided to give him a call to accept the pastorate of the Presbyterian church. There were thirty-two persons present, twenty-eight of them made voluntary subscriptions amounting to four hundred and thirty-eight dollars, which was increased to five hundred and one within an hour. This was then thought to be a very liberal support when compared with previous subscriptions, which had never exceeded one hundred dollars per annum for Presbyterian preaching, besides the missionary's stipend. On the 27th of the same month a subscription was started to build a Presbyterian church edifice. The first place selected was on ground partly covered by the writer's residence on Ridge Row, and grading was commenced under the superintendence of the late John W. Moore. Upon further consideration it was decided to locate the building where it now stands, on Washington avenue between Lackawanna avenue and Spruce street.

Sunday evening, November 25, 1849, Rev. John Dorrance, of Wilkes-Barre, presiding, a regular call was unanimously made out for the Rev. Delville Mitchell to accept the pastorate of the Presbyterian church. Mr. Mitchell having accepted the call, Wednesday evening April 17, 1850, "the pastoral relation between Rev. J. D. Mitchell and the Presbyterian church in this place was constituted by the Presbytery of Luzerne. The Rev. P. E. Stevenson, of Wyoming, preached from John iii : 33 ; Rev. John Dorrance, of Wilkes-Barre, presided, proposed the constitutional questions and gave the charge to the congregation. Rev. T. P. Hunt, of Wyoming, gave the charge to the pastor. A large congregation attended upon the solemn services, which were held in the Odd Fellows' Hall. On April 29, 1851, Mr. W. W. Manness commenced raising the First Presbyterian church edifice ; on September 30 the steeple, and on November 26 put the bell in its place, it being the first bell put up between Carbondale and Wilkes-Barre. On November 27, it was first used for assembling a congregation to worship, it being Thanksgiving Day, and the services were held in the Odd Fellows' Hall. From that day to this the sound of "the church-going bell" has been heard here regularly on Sunday. The church edifice was dedicated by the pastor, September 19, 1852. The cost of this church, for the main body and steeple, was about $15,000. The firm of Scrantons & Platt gave the lot, 155 feet front by 150 feet deep. The general and special partners contributed personally $3,200.00, and their non-resident friends $335.00. Scrantons & Platt deducted from the indebtedness of the church to the firm $5,128.62.

STATEMENT.

Total cost of church $15,000.00
General and special contribu-
    tions, personally . . . $3,200.00
Their non-resident friends .   335.00
Scrantons & Platt . . . .   5,128.62—   8,663.62
                            ———————

Balance paid by congregation and locally, $6,336.38

Since then the congregation has built the parsonage, added the wings to the church in December, 1859, built the lecture room, and put in the organ.

The Methodists, doubtless, like the Presbyterians and Baptists, had for many years considered this as one of their missionary fields or outposts. They had the " Village Chapel "—heretofore referred to—and irregular preaching in it, which the writer attended from November, 1845, to the organization of the First Presbyterian Church, October 14, 1848. The following is from Bishop Simpson's Cyclopedia of Methodism :

"Scranton—The first Methodist Society was organized in 1840 in connection with Pittston circuit and a church edifice erected in 1842 ; in 1854 it was organized as a station," by which it would appear that Scranton was considered as a part of the parish of Pittston, as the Presbyterians years before considered it a part of the parish of Wilkes-Barre. After many inquiries of Methodists and others, it appears by their minutes and records, that the first steps taken towards the organization of a Methodist church in Scranton, was on August 2, 1854, when a meeting of the "male members of the M. E. Church"—of what place or places is not stated—was held. The following persons were elected Trustees, were directed to obtain a charter : John Major, John M. Washington, Thomas Biesecker, John R. Soucks, F. M. Etting, John H. Coleman, Barton Mott, Erastus Smith and William Silkman. A. H. Schoonmaker was the secretary. These Trustees were all Scrantonians, except Erastus Smith who lived in Lackawanna, and William Silkman who lived in Providence. A. H. Schoonmaker was their clergyman. The charter was signed August 9, 1854, the Trustees elected on the 2nd inst. being named in the charter for that purpose.

The two following are copied from the Conference minutes :

"Scranton, 1854, First Quarterly Conference
for Scranton and Hyde Park Mission met, Doctor
George Peck presided. John M. Washington was
chosen secretary." That with quotation marks is
the first entry and all there is of the minutes of
the meeting.

"Scranton, October 28, 1854, Second Quarterly
Conference for Scranton and Hyde Park Mission
met, Rev. George Peck presiding. A. L. Horn
was chosen secretary. Members present—A. H.
Schoonmaker, pastor; local preachers, Noah
Davis and A. L. Horn; leaders, N. Davis and A.
L. Horn; stewards, N. Davis, John Coleman, J.
M. Washington, Thomas Pearce, William Varnes
and A. L. Horn."

April 18, 1855. At a meeting of this date, the
pastor, A. H. Schoonmaker, also secretary *pro tem.*,
stated that the Lackawanna Iron and Coal Co. had
proposed to take the "Village Chapel" lot, 100
feet front by 112 feet deep, and give three lots
fronting on Adams, 110 feet front by 150 feet deep
and pay the church $1,700; the company to have
the old chapel. A committee was appointed, J. M.
Washington, David Kemmerer and Noah Davis,
"with the instruction to obtain, if possible, a better bid for them and retain the old church, at least
until the basement of the new one is ready for
use." April 25, 1855. At a meeting held this date,

it was voted that " we accept the offer made by the Iron Co., on condition that they pay us $2,000 difference between the lots, and also that we be permitted to occupy the old church at least six months or until we get the basement of the new one finished." The present M. E. Church edifice on Adams avenue near Lackawanna, was begun between the 6th and 16th of September, 1855.

January 8, 1855, the churches here this date were : First Presbyterian, on Washington avenue ; St. Luke's Protestant Episcopal, on Penn avenue ; " Village Chapel," Lackawanna and Adams avenues ; Welsh Calvinistic Methodist—Rome street —west end, later moved to River street. (Entry April 1, 1855): The First Roman Catholic, easterly end of Rome street, not then used for church purposes ; The Second Roman Catholic Church, on the corner of Franklin avenue and Spruce street.

BAPTISTS.

Mr. Edward L. Bailey in his "History of the Abington Baptist Association " states, that as early as 1794, Rev. William Bishop, a Baptist, lived in Hyde Park and that he was pastor of the Pittston church, and " a Baptist church, however, was reorganized at Pittston in the autumn of 1833. William K. Mott, pastor of this church, preached occasionally at Hyde Park and baptized a number of converts into the fellowship of the Pittston church." He further states that "the brethren and sisters living at Hyde Park and vicinity, however, finally decided to organize as an independent church. The council of recognition was convened at that place, September 12, 1849; Rev. John Miller acted as moderator and Rev. Silas Finn acting as clerk. Twenty three persons from their respective churches received fellowship at the Hyde Park Baptist church. Rev. William K. Mott was one of the constituent members and pastor of the church. Messrs. E. A. Atherton and J. C. Dunn were chosen deacons of the church."

The Welsh Baptists purchased lot 5 in block 34 on Mifflin avenue, January 1, 1855, and on December 23, of the same year, dedicated a brick edifice they had erected thereon as a house of wor ship. This building now belongs to and is used by the German Lutherans, who have lately added a steeple and made other improvements to it. Elder William K. Mott, of Hyde Park, occupied Odd Fellows' Hall for Baptist services a few times between May 30, 1858, and March, 1859. He had formerly preached occasionally in the "Village Chapel." Mr. Bailey states : "The public recognition of this church (Scranton) took place in the

·Odd Fellows' Hall. Twenty-five brethren and sisters had on the preceding week, August 18th, at the house of Nathaniel Halstead, organized themselves into a church by a unanimous resolution, and by adopting articles of faith and a church covenant." The writer was treasurer of the Odd Fellows' Hall and rented it to the Baptists and all others using it, from its erection until taken down.

This church with its Sunday school occupied the Odd Fellows' Hall from August 1, 1859, to March 1, 1861, and afterwards Washington Hall on Penn avenue. On May 13, 1864, lots 12, 13 and 14 in block 64, on Penn avenue, were purchased and a brick church built thereon which has since been enlarged and very much improved both inside and out. Basement first used for a festival, June 20, 1865—the upper part not ready to use.

The Welsh Congregationalists bought lot 2 in block 28, on Mifflin avenue, July 31, 1854, and built a wooden church upon it in the same year, which they used a few years and then sold. It is now used for dwellings.

The German Presbyterian Church on Hickory street, occupying lots 17 and 19, block 1, worshipped in the Odd Fellows' Hall from 1852 to January 1, 1858. The organization by the Presbytery took place in the hall, June 25, 1856. During this year the Lackawanna Iron and Coal Co.

presented the congregation with one lot and the members purchased the other. The corner stone of the edifice was laid September 5, 1857, and it was dedicated November 6, 1859. The late William E. Dodge, of New York, presented the bell to the congregation. The attendance has so increased that it has been found necessary to purchase the adjoining lot to which it is proposed to remove the church building for temporary use, and on the present site build a much larger stone edifice, and when finished use the old building for Sunday school and other church purposes.

The first Protestant Episcopal Church service in Scranton of which I have any knowledge, was held August 29, 1848, in the "Village Chapel." It was conducted by Bishop Potter, who was brought here from Salem by Judge Pettebone. The next day Mr. John S. Dewey, a bookkeeper of Scrantons & Platt, took him to Wilkes-Barre.

St. Luke's Church and congregation occupied the Odd Fellows' Hall from October 24, 1852, to July 24, 1853. The church was organized August 5, 1851, at the residence of Mr. Charles Swift, formerly of Easton, Pa. Rev. John Long, rector; E. Hitchcock and J. C. Burgess, wardens; B. H. Throop, M. D., Charles Swift, L. N. Clarke, E. S. M. Hill and J. Kirlin, vestrymen. The firm of Scrantons & Platt gave the church authorities lots

26 and 27 in block 30, on Penn avenue—the Lack-awanna Iron and Coal Co., which was organized soon after, made the deed for them. The corner stone of the church building was laid April 19, 1863, "with ceremonies appropriate to the occasion." The services were conducted by Rev. John Long, the rector, assisted by Messrs. Miles, of Wilkes-Barre ; Skinner, of New Milford, and Mendelhall, of Salem. Ten other clergymen of the Episcopal Church being present. The church was consecrated by Bishop Potter, November 13, 1853. Doctor Throop presented the church with a bell which was first used May 22, 1859.

Mr. Platt intended to enlarge these notes but was prevented from doing so by the illness and death of his wife, who died July 4, 1887. Shortly after he was stricken with paralysis and died November 15, 1887. At the request of friends they are now published as he left them, by his children.

JOSEPH C., ELLA J. AND FRANK E. PLATT.

Scranton, Pa., October, 1889.